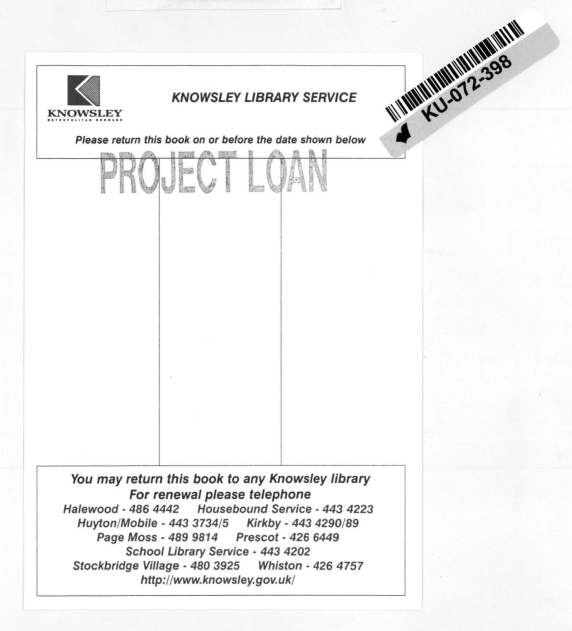

Materials

Wood

Chris Oxlade

H www.heinemann.co.uk/library
Visit our website to find out more information about **Heinemann Library** books.

To Order:
Phone 44 (0) 1865 888066
Send a fax to 44 (0) 1865 314091
Visit the Heinemann Library Bookshop at www.heinemann.co.uk/library to browse our catalogue and order online.

First published in Great Britain by Heinemann Library, Halley Court, Jordan Hill, Oxford OX2 8EJ
a division of Reed Educational and Professional Publishing Ltd.
Heinemann is a registered trademark of Reed Educational & Professional Publishing Ltd.

OXFORD MELBOURNE AUCKLAND JOHANNESBURG BLANTYRE
GABORONE IBADAN PORTSMOUTH (NH) USA CHICAGO

Designed by Storeybooks
Originated by Ambassador Litho Ltd.
Printed in Hong Kong / China

ISBN 0 431 12720 4 (hardback)   ISBN 0 431 12727 1 (paperback)
05 04 03 02 01   06 05 04 03 02
10 9 8 7 6 5 4 3 2   10 9 8 7 6 5 4 3 2 1

British Library Cataloguing in Publication Data
 Oxlade, Chris
 Wood. – (Materials)
 1. Wood
 I. Title
 620.1'2

Acknowledgements
Corbis pp.19, /Jack Fields p.29, /Darrell Gulin p.24, /Barry Lewis p.13, /Richard T. Nowitz p.22; Holt p.6; Hutchison p.23; Oxford Scientific Films pp.4, 9, 10, /Michael Fogden p.25; Photodisc pp.15, 26, 27; Still Pictures /Mark Edwards p.11, /Hartmut Schwarzbach p.12; The Builder Group p.8; Trip/Viesti Collection p.18; Tudor Photography pp.5, 7, 14, 17, 20, 21.

Cover photograph reproduced with permission of Robert Harding Picture Library.

Every effort has been made to contact copyright holders of any material reproduced in this book. Any omissions will be rectified in subsequent printings if notice is given to the Publisher.

Contents

You can find words shown in bold, **like this**, in the Glossary.

What is wood?

branch

trunk

Wood is a **natural** material. It
comes from the trunks and branches
of trees. People cut trees down and
chop them into pieces so that they
can use the wood.

Wood is an important material. People make many different things from wood. They are called wooden objects. The things you can see on this page are made from wood.

Different woods

The trunks and branches of a tree are covered in **bark**. Underneath the bark the wood is **grainy**. It has lots of rings or lines in it. Different woods are different colours.

Some trees have wood which is very hard and heavy. Some trees have soft, light wood. Beech is a hard, heavy wood. Balsa is a soft, light wood.

Strong and bendy

Most kinds of wood are strong when you try to squash or bend them. Hard wood is stronger than soft wood. The inside of this building is made with thick pieces of wood.

The young, thin branches of some trees are very bendy. They can bend almost in half without snapping. This can be very useful for making things.

Rotting and burning

When branches break off a tree and fall to the ground, the wood begins to **rot** away. These wooden floorboards are rotting away because they are damp.

Wood does not **melt** when it is heated. But when it gets very hot, it burns. In many parts of the world people collect wood to use as a **fuel** for cooking or for keeping warm.

Growing wood

Most wood for building and making furniture comes from fir trees. The trees are grown for their wood. When they grow big enough, they are cut down.

After the trees are cut down, the branches are chopped off to leave a trunk. The trunks are carried to a **sawmill** where they are cut into large planks.

Working with wood

Wood is a useful material because it is easy to cut into shapes and make into things. A **carpenter** is a person who cuts and shapes wood to make into things. Carpenters use tools such as saws and drills.

This building is made of wood. First the carpenter cuts the wood into different lengths and shapes with an electric saw. Then he joins the pieces together with bolts and screws.

Sheets of wood

Sheets of wood are called boards.
Chipboard is made of small chunks
of wood. The chunks are mixed
with glue and squeezed
together until the glue
sets hard.

Plywood is another kind of board. It is made by gluing thin sheets of hard wood on top of each other. Plywood is very strong and hard-wearing.

Caring for wood

Wood that is used outdoors must be protected from **rotting**. Two or three layers of oily paint stop water reaching the wood's surface.

Fence posts are dipped in special **chemicals** before they are put in the ground. These chemicals are called preservatives. They help to stop the posts rotting.

Looking good

The grainy patterns in wood are often beautiful. They are used for decoration. The wood is made smooth with **sandpaper** and then polished to make the **grain** show up.

Pieces of wood with different colours can be put next to each other to make patterns. Some wooden furniture and other things used in houses have patterns made from small pieces of wood.

Local wood

People who live in places where there are large forests use wood for almost everything they make. Log cabins are built from whole tree trunks.

People who live by rivers in the world's **rainforests** make boats from tree trunks. They dig out the centre of the trunk with axes. These boats are called dug-out canoes.

Animal wood users

Like humans, many animals use wood as a building material. Beavers cut down trees with their sharp front teeth and use them to build **dams** and homes called lodges.

Many birds make nests from dead branches and twigs they collect from the ground. Bowerbirds are expert builders. The male bird builds something called a bower from twigs and grasses to attract a **mate**.

Saving the rainforests

Tropical **rainforests** are full of huge, old trees. They are a very important part of the world, and many animals live there. Every day people cut down thousands of the rainforest trees to get wood.

One way to help save the rainforests from being cut down is to plant more trees. If we get our wood from these planted trees, we do not need to cut down the rainforests.

Fact file

Wood is a **natural** material. It comes from trees, which are a kind of plant.

Wood from a tree feels rough. It has lines in it called the **grain**.

Woods from different kinds of trees are different colours.

Some kinds of wood are heavy and hard. Some are light and soft.

Old, thick pieces of wood are stiff. Young, thin pieces of wood are bendy.

Wood burns when it is heated up.

Wood floats in water.

Wood is not attracted by **magnets**.

Electricity and heat do not flow through wood.

Would you believe it?

There is an aircraft built in 1947 called the *Spruce Goose*. It is the biggest aircraft in the world, even bigger than a modern jumbo jet. It is made completely from wood!

Glossary

bark outer layer of wood on a tree trunk or a branch

carpenter person who works with wood to make things

chemicals special materials that are used in factories and homes to do many jobs, including cleaning and protecting

dam structure that holds back water to make a lake

electricity form of energy. We use electricity to make electric machines work.

fuel substance that people burn to make heat or light, or to make engines work. Wood is a fuel. So are gas and petrol.

grain the pattern of rings and lines inside wood

magnet object that pulls steel and iron objects towards it

mate male or female animal in a pair of animals that have babies together

melt turn from solid to liquid

natural comes from plants, animals or the rocks in the earth

rainforest thick, jungly forest where lots of rain falls

rot go soft and crumbly. Wood rots when it gets damp and tiny animals and plants start living on it.

sandpaper tough paper with grains of sand glued to it. Rubbing wood with sandpaper makes the wood smooth.

sawmill factory where trees are cut into planks with powerful saws

More books to read

Life Cycle of an Oak Tree
Angela Royston
Heinemann Library, 2000

Plants: British Trees
Angela Royston
Heinemann Library, 2000

*Science All Around Me:
Materials*
Karen Bryant-Mole
Heinemann Library, 1996

Science Explorers: Wood
A & C Black, 1999

Find Out About . . . Wood
Henry Pluckrose
Franklin Watts UK

Index

Titles in the *Materials* series include:

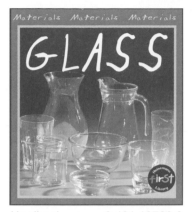

Hardback   0 431 12723 9

Hardback   0 431 12722 0

Hardback   0 431 12725 5

Hardback   0 431 12721 2

Hardback   0 431 12720 4

Hardback   0 431 12724 7

Find out about the other titles in this series on our website www.heinemann.co.uk/library